IRELAND

A PICTURE MEMORY

Text
Finn Trehearn

Captions
Fleur Robertson

Design
Teddy Hartshorn

Photography
Colour Library Books Ltd

Commissioning Editor
Andrew Preston

Publishing Assistant
Edward Doling

Editorial
Gill Waugh
Pauline Graham

Production
Ruth Arthur
Sally Connolly
David Proffit
Andrew Whitelaw

Director of Production
Gerald Hughes

Director of Publishing
David Gibbon

CLB 2524
This 1991 edition published by Crescent Books,
distributed by Outlet Book Company, Inc., a Random House Company,
40 Engelhard Avenue, Avenel, New Jersey 07001

Random House
New York • Toronto • London • Sydney • Auckland

Printed and bound in Singapore

ISBN 0 517 05319 5

8 7 6 5 4 3 2

IRELAND

A PICTURE MEMORY

CRESCENT BOOKS
NEW YORK / AVENEL, NEW JERSEY

For thousands of years, Ireland was the edge of the known world. The island lies on the most westerly tip of the vast Eurasian landmass. To the west, there is nothing except the Atlantic Ocean. To the east there is another small island, Britain, and then beyond that the great North European plain runs away to the Ural Mountains. Beyond the Urals, Siberia folds around the curve of the world until it reaches the Bering Strait, almost touching Alaska. For most of human history, therefore, Ireland was at the very edge of the known world.

The Romans, who went just about everywhere, never bothered with Ireland. After all, everyone knew that Ireland was just an island on the edge of nowhere. Everyone, that is, except the Irish, who were certain that there was something out there beyond the ocean. They proved it, too. It is widely believed that Irishman St Brendan discovered America a thousand years before Columbus sailed.

Like St Brendan, the Irish have always been curious about the outside world. They have not always been willing emigrants, but they have been remarkably successful ones. Today, in the United States alone, forty million people are proud to claim Irish descent, and all around the world there is ample testimony to the intelligence, hard work and determination of Irish people.

Ireland is her people. But the Irish people are, in turn, formed by the magnificent combination of landscape and climate that is the island of Ireland. The country is a mixture of magnificent mountains, rolling and fertile plains and clear, unpolluted rivers and lakes. Although the Irish often complain about the weather, they are in fact blessed with one of the most benign climates in the world. There are no extremes of heat or cold, and when the sun shines, it is a paradise.

Perhaps it is this temperate and gentle climate that gives the country and the people their character. Ireland is relaxed and easy-going, not given to hurry or excess and always ready with a welcome for the stranger. *Céad mile fáilte* is the traditional Gaelic greeting: a hundred thousand welcomes. So it has always been and always will be.

That ready greeting, that hand extended to the visitor, is the modern version of Ireland's eternal curiosity about other people and other places. For it is, as millions of visitors to Ireland over the years can verify, something sincere and genuine. It is neither forced nor manufactured. When an Irish person tells you that you are welcome, it is meant from the heart. Like every country, Ireland has its faults but cynicism in its people is not one of them.

So relax and enjoy the country where time goes more slowly and the people are more friendly and life is gentler than anywhere else you have ever been. See the magnificent and majestic scenery of Kerry and Cork, with Killarney – 'heaven's reflection' – at its centre. Visit rugged Connemara and, just to the north of it, the lakes of Mayo and the Yeats country. Travel the stunningly beautiful coast of Donegal, or the Glens of Antrim, two of Ireland's best kept secrets. Marvel at the rich river valleys of the southeast and the rolling, fertile fields of the Golden Vale rippling across north Munster from east Tipperary to the very borders of Kerry itself. And don't forget the towns and cities: Dublin, one of the truly great world capitals, sophisticated and yet small enough not to have lost its human dimension; Belfast, a fine Victorian city surrounded by the most gorgeous countryside; Cork, the Venice of the south; Galway, a centre of learning and the arts, with its fabled bay; Limerick, standing proudly at the head of the Shannon estuary – the list goes on.

So welcome to Ireland: *céad mile fáilte*. Ireland is no longer at the edge of the world. It is, in a strange way, the centre of the world. Or at least it is the centre of that world in which people strive to lead a good and decent life, in which human values prevail and where no one is ever too busy to throw you a wave or a greeting. Enjoy it, and when your visit ends you will discover, like so many visitors before you, that you are just a little lonely leaving Ireland. Because Ireland is a kind of home for all of us, a home from home for the human heart.

Left: part of the 100-metre frontage of Queen Elizabeth I's 'College of the Holy and Undivided Trinity', today better known simply as Trinity College, Dublin, the capital's most renowned institute of learning. Here can be seen that world-famous masterpiece of illumination, the Book of Kells, a Latin text of the four Gospels, which lies in the Long Room of the college's library. A leaf of this glisteningly beautiful book is turned daily. The college was founded in 1592 by Queen Elizabeth I and can boast Oliver Goldsmith, Edmund Burke and Oscar Wilde among its graduates. Below: the General Post Office on O'Connell Street. To Irishmen, this building is always known by its initials. It was here that the 1916 Easter Rising took place when its leader, Patrick Pearse and a band of some 150 armed men, simply walked in to the GPO and ordered everybody out. Pearse then read the Proclamation of the Irish Republic and awaited the British troops. They came, and within a fortnight the ringleaders of the rebellion had been executed. With their deaths the dream of an independent Ireland was born. A copy of the Proclamation is displayed in the GPO. Facing page: (top) the Four Courts on the River Liffey and (bottom and overleaf) the bridge and street named after Daniel O'Connell.

Facing page: St Patrick's Cathedral, Dublin, one of the oldest
places of worship in the capital. Dedicated in 1192, the cathedral
has been restored many times and since the Reformation has
belonged to the Church of Ireland. Jonathan Swift, the renowned
satirist who was Dean of the cathedral for over thirty years, is
buried here. Above: the ornate and gilt-laden Throne Room, part
of the lavish State Apartments designed for English viceroys in
Dublin Castle and (below) contrasting simplicity in Ireland's
oldest public library, Marsh's Library, where patrons' reading
cages – designed to prevent pilferage – are still in place. The
library was founded in 1701 by Archbishop Marsh. Right: the
appropriately named Long Room, Trinity College, Dublin, lined
with marble busts of the college's famous alumni. Here can be
found four Shakespeare folios, as well as the Book of Kells.

Above: a splendid door and (below left) an ornate floor, typical of the surroundings that provide elegant backdrops for the exhibits in Dublin's National Museum (below). Above left: *The Wrestlers*, a copy of a marble sculpture by Piamontini in the National Gallery, which boasts works by Rembrandt, El Greco and Degas, as well as a number by Irish artists such as Jack B. Yeats and Walter Osborne. Facing page: the National Library, a comprehensive treasure house of information about Ireland.

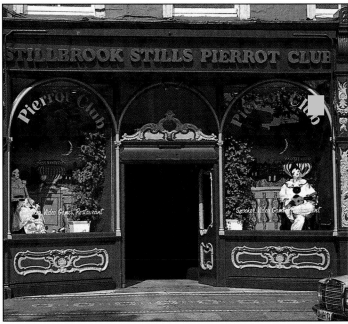

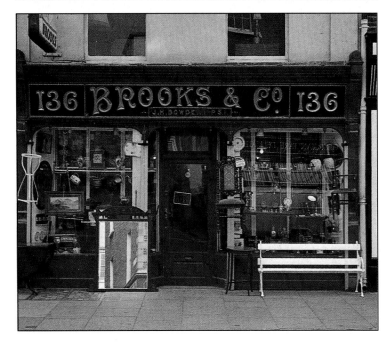

Facing page: Dublin shops and pubs. Unlike English pubs, Irish
bars have no signs outside and, to the uninitiated, they look like
shops. Once inside, though, it is clear where one is (below).

Right: marigolds in Merrion Square, where Yeats once lived. Below: Dublin's Grand Canal, an eighteenth-century waterway which connects Dublin Bay with the mighty River Shannon. Now closed to commercial traffic, it has become a place for quiet walks, seeming almost rural in nature along some of its length. Equally restful is the city's huge park, Phoenix Park (below right and bottom right) – the largest enclosed park in any European city. It contains, among other features, a herd of fallow deer, a zoo, a polo ground and the residence of the Irish premier.

Below: a horse grazes in the Vale of Clara (left), and (below left) autumn tints the surroundings of the 1000-year-old Round Tower at Glendalough Monastery, both in County Wicklow.

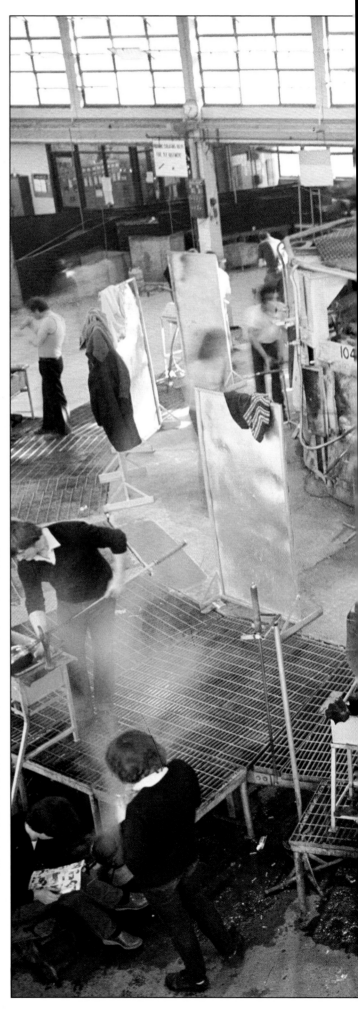

Right and top: glass-making at the Waterford Glass works. The factory can be visited during working hours, when informative guides lead the way through the processes of glass blowing, polishing and cutting. A display of crystal produced at the works can be examined in the entrance hall, where a magnificent collection of intricate chandeliers (above) presides over all.

Above left: the ruins of Muckross Abbey and (above) well-preserved Muckross House, both near Killarney in County Kerry. Left and below: Ashford Castle on the shores of Lough Corrib near Cong, County Mayo. The castle, once owned by the Guinness family, is today a hotel that holds the distinction of having been thought one of the best in the British Isles by Egon Ronay. At its gates lie the ruins of a twelfth-century Augustinian abbey (facing page bottom right), part of which has been reconstructed. Facing page: (top left, top right and bottom left) Blarney Castle, which lies northwest of Cork. One of the most famous ruins in Ireland, Blarney Castle is visited annually by thousands wishing to kiss the Blarney Stone and so, according to the legend, acquire the gift of eloquence. Overleaf: Cork pastureland.

Cork (these pages), the second largest city in the Republic of Ireland, lies on an island in the River Lee and has been been christened the 'Paris of Ireland' for its beauty. Below: Cork's Father Mathew Memorial Church, named for the founder of the Irish temperance movement. Overleaf: St Colman's Cathedral overlooks the harbour in Cobh, County Cork.

Facing page: a rainbow – a common sight in this land of showers – arching over St Mary's Cathedral in Killarney, County Kerry. Below: fishing boats huddle in Dingle Harbour, the most westerly harbour in Europe, County Kerry. Bottom left: Dingle's unassuming Main Street contrasts with the bustle of Castle Street (bottom right) in Tralee, Kerry's industrial centre.

Left: foaming seas off Coumeenoole Strand on the Dingle Peninsula (these pages), County Kerry. The Peninsula has as its spine the rounded peaks of the Slieve Mish range. This chain stretches the strip of land nearly fifty kilometres out to sea and holds, at its tip, the westernmost habitations of Europe. Bottom: the view from Smerwick Harbour towards Kilmalkedar.

These pages: the Dingle Peninsula, County Kerry. The beaches in the west of Ireland are some of the finest in Europe, but they remain undisturbed because, although the country is washed by the Gulf Stream, a dip in the sea remains a bracing experience. Nevertheless, on a sunny day a beach as fine as Coumeenoole Strand (bottom and right) will draw numerous visitors.

In Ireland, ruins and ancient remains may be found around any corner. On the Dingle Peninsula (these pages) the stone that is such a feature of the landscape of Kerry has been used to fashion walls and houses that seem as natural as their surroundings. Bottom left: the Gallarus Oratory, a remarkable survival from early Christian times, which lies near Ballyferriter.

Left and below: the undeniably romantic ramparts of the Cliffs of Moher, which defy the Atlantic north of Liscannor in County Clare. In places they rise sheer for over 200 metres. Bottom: a blacksmith uses the age-old tools of his trade at his forge in Bunratty, County Clare. In Ireland, where there's a horse to be found in most villages, the smith is an important man.

Facing page: a fisherman waits hopefully beside the torrent of the Owenriff River in County Galway. Above: white water spills from Ballynahinch Lough and (right) hay dries in Roundstone, both in Joyce Country, Connemara, one of the loneliest and loveliest regions of Ireland. Below: a solitary cottage near Leenane, County Galway, which could belong to the last, rather than the present, century. Overleaf: Lough Corrib, County Galway.

Above: a traditional Irish sailing boat, known as a hooker, in Carna, County Galway. Such vessels often dock in Roundstone harbour (above left and left), Bertraghboy Bay (below left) and other Galway ports of call. Below: a cockerel struts in front of Maumeen Lough and the Twelve Bens, or Pins, of Connemara beyond. These peaks, which change colour with the light and the season, are part of the Benna Beola range. Facing page: a lone rowing boat lies in shadow as sunshine falls on the green shores of Westport Bay near Murrisk in County Mayo.

Below and bottom left: tranquil water reflects a rich blend of greens and blues – the colours of the Irish countryside – at Killary Harbour, which forms part of the county boundary between Mayo and Galway. Below left: donkeys graze and gaze beside Kingstown Bay (left), which lies west of Clifden in Connemara, a region better known for the world-famous Connemara pony than for these humble beasts of burden.

Below: a white statue of St Patrick, the patron saint of Ireland, overlooks Clew Bay at the foot of Croagh Patrick, a 762-metre-high mountain in County Mayo. A conical peak, the mountain is considered to be holy, since legend has it that Saint Patrick spent forty days here in prayer and fasting for the people of Ireland. Bottom right: Ashleagh Falls, near Leenane, and (remaining pictures) timeless rural scenes, all in County Mayo.

Facing page centre right: a Donegal donkey. Remaining pictures: Donegal men, working and resting. Though farming may look idyllic, it is hard work – especially at haymaking and harvest.

Left: Adare Manor, a Neo-Gothic mansion built by the third Earl of Dunraven, who also built a row of cottages in Adare, County Limerick, for his tenants. Unlike many Englishmen, the earl was a popular landlord; his son went on to instigate the 1903 act that enabled tenants to buy the land they farmed. Below: the River Blackwater, County Meath, and (bottom) Birr Castle, County Offaly. Overleaf: the Cooley Peninsula, County Louth.

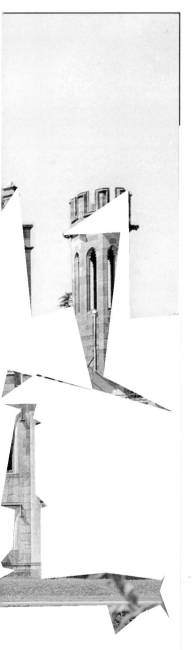

Above: a waterfall in the Glencar Lakes area of County Leitrim and (below) Lough Key Forest Park, one of many state-owned recreation areas in County Sligo. Above left: the limestone rock formation known as the Wishing Arch, visible from the Antrim coast road, a route which affords the walker spectacular views of brown moorlands, white limestone, black basalt, red sandstone and blue sea. The road, a notable engineering achievement, was built in 1834 to provide work for famine victims and opened up an area whose inhabitants had previously found it easier to travel by sea to Scotland than overland to the rest of Ireland. Left: golfers on the green in County Monaghan. Golf is a national passion and is played by everyone in Ireland sufficiently interested to buy a set of clubs; the country is dotted with golf courses. Facing page: the rope bridge at Carrick-a-rede, near Ballintoy, County Antrim. Visitors view this slim bridge, which is taken down during the winter months, when the winds become severe, with some trepidation. Locals, however, happily cross it, maintaining their balance despite the considerable sway their speed produces. Below left: fishing boats cluster in Kilkeel Harbour after braving the fierce Irish Sea. Kilkeel, in County Down, lies at the foot of the beautiful Mountains of Mourne. Overleaf: sea pinks brighten an overcast day at White Rocks on the Antrim coast.